THE UPDATED PATAGONIA TRAVEL GUIDE 2023

Discover Patagonia's Best Hikes, Tours, And Attractions: A Visual Tour Of The Stunning Landscape And Rich Culture Of Southern Argentina And Chile.

Julia Howard

Copyright © 2023 Julia Howard

All rights reserved. No part of this publication may be reproduced, distributed, or transmitted in any form or by any means, including photocopying, recording, or other electronic or mechanical methods, without the prior written permission of the publisher, except in the case of brief quotations embodied in critical reviews and certain other non-commercial uses permitted by copyright law.

TABLE OF CONTENTS.

INTRODUCTION 5

CHAPTER 1 9

    Welcome to Patagonia 9

    Making Travel Arrangements to Patagonia 11

CHAPTER 2 16

    Arriving In Patagonia 16

    Airlines and Flights 17

    Options for Overland Travel in Patagonia 20

    Conditions for Entry and Visas 25

CHAPTER 3 29

    Patagonia Exploration 29

    Various Places and Regions 30

    National Parks 33

CHAPTER 4 43

Dining and Lodging 43

The Various Accommodation Options 44

Eateries and Cafés. 51

CHAPTER 5 55

Cities in Patagonia 55

CHAPTER 6 59

Hiking in Patagonia 59

Hiking Trails 59

Trekking Equipment 60

Preparation: 61

CHAPTER 7 63

Culture of Patagonia 63

Celebrations and Festivals: 65

CHAPTER 8 67

Hints and Concluding Suggestions 67

Conclusion 70

INTRODUCTION

Argentina and Chile both share Patagonia, which is located at the southernmost point of South America.

Patagonia is a popular vacation destination for daring tourists from all over the globe because of its breathtaking scenery, dramatic natural features, and distinctive fauna.

Patagonia offers a variety of activities to offer, whether you're searching for a strenuous hike through the Andes, a tranquil boat trip around glacier lakes, or just an opportunity to relax and enjoy the surroundings' grandeur in its natural state.

Patagonia may be challenging and distant to explore without enough planning and preparedness. Significant wilderness areas are also present there. As a result, everyone considering traveling to Patagonia needs to have a trustworthy and comprehensive travel guide.

Regardless of your level of travel knowledge, having access to reliable and current information about the area's attractions, accommodation alternatives, transit options, and cultural traditions may significantly improve your vacation.

My Patagonia travel guide strives to be that crucial resource for anybody considering traveling to this amazing area.

This book provides a comprehensive overview of all you need to know to make the most of your Patagonia vacation.

It relies on my considerable experience visiting Patagonia and my love for teaching others about its delights.

From the jagged Andean peaks to the huge pampas grasslands, this book provides comprehensive information on the top attractions in the region. Among the famous natural beauties I'll show you around are the Perito Moreno Glacier, the Torres del Paine National

Park, and the Tierra del Fuego archipelago. So that you can concentrate on appreciating Patagonia's beauty while traveling, I'll provide useful advise along the way on everything from making an itinerary to packing the appropriate gear.

However, Patagonia offers more than simply breathtaking landscapes and outdoor activities. The area is also fascinatingly influenced by both native and European cultures, making it rich in cultural traditions and history.

You will learn about the native Mapuche people in this introduction to the history and culture of the region as well as the daring adventurers who first explored the arid terrain.

You'll learn strategies for overcoming any language or cultural barriers you may come across while traveling, as well as the ideal locations to try the regional food and sip the area's well-known wines.

My Patagonia travel guide is your go-to source for anything Patagonia, whether you're organizing a trip for the entire family or just you and your significant other.

This book will help you maximize your vacation and create memories that will last a lifetime with its comprehensive insider tips and useful recommendations.

Prepare to be amazed by Patagonia's breathtaking splendor by packing your baggage and donning your hiking boots!

CHAPTER 1

Welcome to Patagonia

At the southernmost point of South America, you will find Patagonia, a big and breathtaking environment. Patagonia is a popular travel destination for outdoorsmen and environment enthusiasts because of its breathtaking scenery, diverse wildlife, and distinctive culture.

Patagonia is a region that straddles Chile and Argentina and is home to beautiful forests, windswept plains, mighty mountains, and enormous glaciers.

Jagged peaks rising up from dazzling lakes and glaciers tumbling into azure fjords are just a few of the area's magnificent natural features.

The Andes mountain range, which borders Patagonia on its western side, is among its most recognizable natural characteristics. Aconcagua, which soars to a mind-blowing 22,841 feet in height, is one of the world's tallest peaks and is found in the Andes. (6,962 meters).

Visitors to Patagonia have the option of taking a slower approach by enjoying a scenic drive along the renowned Route 40, or they may choose to hike along one of the numerous paths that crisscross the highlands to take in the breathtaking views.

The glaciers of Patagonia, some of the biggest and most magnificent in the world, are another noteworthy feature of the region.

Due to the spectacular ice formations and opportunity to see ice calving episodes, the Perito Moreno Glacier in Argentina is especially well-known. To get right up and personal with these natural beauties, visitors may stroll over the ice or enjoy boat trips.

But there is more to Patagonia than simply the splendor of nature. Additionally, the area is home to a rich cultural legacy that has been influenced by the native peoples who have lived on this territory for countless years. Indigenous villages in the area may now be visited by tourists who are interested in learning about their traditional way of life, which is based on subsistence farming and a close relationship with the soil.

The gaucho culture, which is a distinctive fusion of Spanish and indigenous traditions, is another aspect of Patagonia's indigenous culture that sets it apart from other regions.

The colorful ponchos and caps that residents wear, as well as the robust food that includes grilled meats and local cheeses, are all remnants of the gauchos' impact on the area. The gauchos were expert riders and ranchers.

Making Travel Arrangements to Patagonia

Due to the size and variety of the area, organizing a vacation to Patagonia may be both fascinating and difficult. Patagonia is a region that includes parts of Chile and Argentina and is home to a variety of scenic landscapes, quaint settlements, and outdoor pursuits.

A detailed preparation process is necessary in order to guarantee a seamless and memorable vacation. The planning process for a vacation to Patagonia will be covered in this guide.

Choose A Spending Limit.

Establishing your budget is one of the first preparation tasks for your trip to Patagonia. The price of a vacation to Patagonia might vary greatly depending on your travel preferences, spending capacity, and length of stay.

To get a feel of how much money you'll need to spend, it's a good idea to look up the area's average expenditures for travel, lodging, and activities.

Set A Departure Time.

Seasonal variations in the climate in Patagonia have a big influence on travel plans. Your plans for activities and the areas you wish to see will determine the ideal time to visit Patagonia.

For instance, in southern Patagonia, the summer months (December to February) are perfect for outdoor activities like trekking, while the shoulder seasons (September to November and March to May) provide less tourists and milder temperatures for seeing the area's cities and towns.

Decide Where You'll Go.

There are innumerable places to visit in the huge territory of Patagonia. Finding out the parts of Patagonia you wish to tour requires thorough study about the many regions, national parks, and cities.

El Chalten, Bariloche, Ushuaia, and Puerto Natales are a few of the well-known places to visit.

Establish A Schedule.

Planning your itinerary is necessary after choosing your locations. Take into account your available time and the route you'll take to go from one place to another. Will you drive a rental vehicle or utilize public transportation? Taking a ship or a flight between regions? To account for unforeseen delays or weather changes, it's also crucial to leave some flexibility in your schedule.

Reserving a Room

From opulent resorts to inexpensive hostels and campsites, Patagonia offers a wide range of lodging alternatives.

Researching and reserving lodging in advance is an excellent idea, particularly during the busiest times of year, to guarantee availability and prevent disappointment.

Find Out More about Outdoor Pursuits

Patagonia's breathtaking natural beauty and outdoor recreation opportunities are among its key attractions. There are various opportunities to explore the wildness of the area, from horseback riding and kayaking to hiking and trekking. It's a smart idea to conduct some research on the various outdoor activities that are offered and to reserve any guided tours or equipment rentals in advance.

Determine the Necessary Visas

Checking visa requirements and making sure you have all the required papers in place is crucial if you're going to Patagonia from outside of your country.

You may have to get a visa in advance of your trip depending on your nationality.

Pack Properly.

For your vacation to Patagonia, it's essential to pack sensibly.

Due to the variable nature of the area's temperature, it is imperative to pack warm and waterproof clothes, durable footwear, and vital outdoor equipment. A first aid kit and any essential prescriptions are also a good idea to include.

CHAPTER 2

Arriving In Patagonia

With a variety of means of transportation available to visit this isolated and stunning area at the southern tip of South America, getting to Patagonia is an experience in and of itself.

There are various routes to get to Patagonia, each providing a different viewpoint on this breathtaking environment, whether you're going from inside Argentina or Chile or arriving from farther beyond.

This guide will examine the different modes of transportation to assist you in planning your trip to Patagonia, including planes, overland travel, ferries, and cruises.

Airlines and Flights

One of the easiest and most popular methods to go to Patagonia is by flight, with numerous well-known airlines operating in both Chile and Argentina.

Despite being a distant area, Patagonia has excellent flight connections to important towns in both nations, making it simpler than ever to go to this spectacular location.

Patagonia Airports

There are a number of airports in Patagonia, some of which are situated in the towns of Punta Arenas, Puerto Natales, El Calafate, and Ushuaia.

It is now simpler to get to Patagonia from other regions of South America and abroad because to the variety of local and international flights that are available at these airports.

Large Airlines That Fly To Patagonia

Patagonia is served by a number of significant airlines, several of which provide flights from important Argentine and Chilean cities as well as connections from other international locations.

LATAM Airlines, Aerolineas Argentinas, Sky Airlines, JetSMART, and LAN Airlines are a few of the most well-known airlines that fly to Patagonia.

To locate the finest alternatives for your trip plans, it's crucial to explore several airlines and their itineraries.

Purchasing a Flight to Patagonia

Plan ahead and reserve early when purchasing tickets for flights to Patagonia to guarantee availability and lock in the best prices.

It's a good idea to research costs and book early to save money on flights to Patagonia since they may be pricey, particularly during the busy season.

You may customize your travel arrangements to meet your unique demands thanks to the affordable prices and adaptable booking choices provided by a number of online travel firms and airline websites.

Comparing Domestic and International Travel

It's important to think about whether you'll be flying domestically or internationally while visiting Patagonia. If you're traveling from anywhere other than Argentina or Chile, you may have to fly internationally to get there, which might be more costly and need extra paperwork like passports or visas.

There are several daily flights to major cities in Patagonia on domestic flights inside Argentina and Chile, which are often more convenient and less expensive.

Traveling through Patagonia

After you arrive in Patagonia, you must plan your transportation once you are there.

While traveling by plane is a practical method to visit well-known towns and locations, travelling about Patagonia may be difficult, particularly in rural regions.

While some visitors choose guided excursions or treks, the majority prefer to hire a vehicle or take the bus to explore the area at their own speed.

To guarantee a smooth and comfortable vacation, it's crucial to explore transportation alternatives and make advance plans.

Patagonia may be reached quickly and easily by planes and airlines, since numerous big airlines fly to and from the area's airports.

It's now simpler than ever to tour this breathtaking and inaccessible area thanks to meticulous preparation and research that will help you identify the finest flying alternatives for your itinerary and financial constraints.

Options for Overland Travel in Patagonia

In order to fully experience the spectacular scenery and culture of Patagonia, overland travel is a well-liked method of exploration. Patagonia offers a variety of overland transportation choices, each with its own advantages and difficulties, ranging from buses and railroads to rental automobiles and camper vans.

Patagonia Bus Service

Several bus companies provide frequent trips connecting major towns and locations, making buses a well-liked and reasonably priced mode of transportation in Patagonia.

Buses provide breathtaking views of the area's surroundings and the chance to mingle with residents and other passengers, despite the fact that they might be slower than other forms of transportation.

A comfortable ride is made possible by the fact that many buses in Patagonia include facilities like air conditioning and comfy seats.

Patagonia Trains

Trains are a second well-liked mode of overland transportation in Patagonia, with a number of picturesque lines providing breath-taking vistas of the area's surroundings. Even while trains are often more costly than buses, they provide a memorable travel experience, with certain lines offering cozy sleeping cabins and dining carriages.

The Andean Explorer and the La Trochita Old Patagonian Express are two of the most well-known railway lines in Patagonia.

Patagonia Car Rentals

With several car rental businesses providing automobiles in significant towns and airports, renting a car is a well-liked approach to see Patagonia at your own leisure.

Rental vehicles might cost more than other forms of transportation, but they provide you the opportunity to see off-the-beaten-path locations and the flexibility to choose your schedule.

It's crucial to learn about the rules of the road in Patagonia and to be ready for lengthy lengths of off-the-beaten-path, gravel roads.

In Patagonia, Camper Vans

Many rental firms provide camper vans and RVs, which are a well-liked choice for tourists wanting to experience Patagonia's untamed terrain and isolated regions.

The independence to travel at your own speed and the convenience of having your lodging and transportation in one vehicle are two benefits of camper vans.

However, they may be pricey and need thorough planning and preparation, including storing up on food and drink and locating acceptable overnight parking spots.

Patagonia Guided Tours

Another way to go overland in Patagonia is on a guided trip; many tour operators provide packages that include lodging, activities, and transportation. With skilled guides sharing insights into the area's culture and history, guided tours may be a convenient and stress-free way to explore the area.

They may, however, be more costly and less flexible in terms of schedule and activities than other vacation alternatives.

Patagonia's choices for overland travel provide a unique and remarkable approach to experience this breathtaking and far-off area.

To fit your travel preferences and price range, there are a variety of transportation options accessible, including buses, trains, rental vehicles, and camper vans.

To guarantee a successful and pleasurable trip to Patagonia, it's important to do your homework and make advance plans.

Conditions for Entry and Visas

Patagonia is a huge area in South America that includes both Chile and Argentina. Therefore, depending on which part of Patagonia you want to visit, different visa policies and entrance criteria apply.

Argentina

You must make sure you have the required documentation to enter Argentina if you want to go to the Argentinean side of Patagonia.

Argentina does not need a visa for the majority of visitors from the United States, Canada, and many other nations. You must, however, have a passport that is current and has at least a six-month validity from the date of admission.

Additionally, a "reciprocity fee" that differs depending on your country must be paid when you arrive.

Chile

In order to enter Chile, you must have the appropriate documentation if you want to go to the Chilean side of Patagonia.

The majority of visitors from the United States, Canada, and several other nations are also not need to have a visa in order to enter Chile.

You must, however, have a passport that is current and has at least a six-month validity from the date of admission.

A "tourist fee" will also need to be paid upon arrival; it is presently $117 for US citizens and may be made with cash or a credit card.

Transcending the Border

It's crucial to learn the documentation needs and guidelines for each nation if you want to cross the border between Argentina and Chile while in Patagonia.

Although crossing the border is not difficult, you may need to provide documentation of your next destination, such as a bus or airplane ticket. You can also be asked to provide documentation showing where you will stay, that you have travel insurance, and that you have enough money to cover your expenses.

Conditions for COVID-19

Both Argentina and Chile have adopted a number of entrance procedures and limitations in response to the current COVID-19 pandemic to aid in controlling the virus' spread.

It's important to learn about the current admission criteria and limitations for both countries before visiting Patagonia.

This can include giving a negative COVID-19 test result, quarantining after arrival, and submitting health documents and declarations.

Which side of Patagonia you want to visit may affect your ability to enter and get a visa. Before going, it is important to familiarize oneself with the required paperwork and documentation for each nation, as well as to keep abreast of any changes to COVID-19-related entrance criteria or limitations.

You may have a hassle-free and secure vacation to Patagonia by preplanning and making sure you have the required documentation.

CHAPTER 3

Patagonia Exploration

Patagonia is a wonderful destination for nature enthusiasts and adventure seekers because to its spectacular natural scenery, rich animals, and distinctive culture.

There is no lack of breathtaking natural beauties to discover, from the majestic Andes Mountains' towering peaks to the clear lakes and glaciers.

Everyone can find something to enjoy in Patagonia, whether they love hiking, kayaking, skiing, or just soaking in the stunning environment.

We'll look at some of the top methods for discovering and enjoying Patagonia's attractions.

Various Places and Regions

Patagonia is home to a variety of breathtaking natural beauties, including towering peaks, glaciers, wild beaches, and clear lakes. We'll look at some of Patagonia's greatest areas and locations in this guide.

National Park of Torres del Paine in Chile

One of Patagonia's most well-known sites is Torres del Paine National Park, which is situated in the southernmost region of Chilean Patagonia and is a UNESCO Biosphere Reserve.

The park is a haven for hikers, climbers, and environment lovers because to its expansive glaciers, blue lakes, and towering granite peaks.

The W Trek, the O Circuit, and the Mirador Las Torres trek are some of the most well-liked paths in the park.

National Park of Los Glaciares in Argentina

The enormous wilderness region of Los Glaciares National Park, which is situated in the Argentine

Patagonia, is home to several glaciers, including the well-known Perito Moreno Glacier.

In addition, the park is home to Mount Fitz Roy and Cerro Torre, two of the most beautiful summits in the Andes.

The enormous glaciers of the park may be explored by boat or kayak, or visitors can stroll along some of the park's well-known paths, such the Laguna de los Tres trip.

Argentina's Ushuaia.

A little city near Argentina's southernmost point known as the "End of the World" is Ushuaia.

Ushuaia is a well-known entry point to Antarctica and provides a variety of outdoor activities, including skiing, hiking, and kayaking, all while being surrounded by snow-capped mountains and breathtaking rivers.

The adjacent Tierra del Fuego National Park is open for exploration, and boat tours of the Beagle Channel are also available.

Argentine city of El Chaltén

El Chaltén is a little village that is a well-liked base camp for hikers and climbers, and it is tucked away at the foot of the Andes Mountains.

The village is close to Los Glaciares National Park and is encircled by some of Patagonia's most breathtaking mountains, including Mount Fitz Roy and Cerro Torre.

The park's many paths may be explored by visitors, including the Cerro Torre and Laguna de los Tres hikes.

In Chile, Puerto Varas

Puerto Varas, a lovely hamlet with breathtaking views of the Osorno and Calbuco volcanoes, is situated on the beaches of Lake Llanquihue in Chilean Patagonia.

The town's German tradition and architecture may be seen by visitors, and they can also take a boat trip of the neighboring lake.

A well-liked starting point for visiting surrounding sites like the Petrohue Falls or the Vicente Perez Rosales National Park is the town.

There are many natural beauties to discover in the vast and varied area of Patagonia. There are plenty beautiful places to explore, from imposing peaks and glaciers to untainted lakes and wild coasts.

Everyone can find something to enjoy in Patagonia, whether they love hiking, kayaking, skiing, or just soaking in the stunning environment.

National Parks

There is no need to mince words. Few places in the world can match the natural wonders found in South America's southernmost point.

These national parks in Patagonia are ready to steal your breath away when you're wanting to explore.

The National Park of Torres del Paine

Torres del Paine, perhaps the best national park in South America, is a breathtaking example of Patagonia's magnificence. The Paine mountain range's three towering granite peaks, from which the park derives its name, are only one of the many attractions that draw so many visitors each year.

It has a vast 1,810 square kilometers and is renowned for its stunning landscapes, which combine unusual rock formations in its mountains with eye-catching glacial lakes.

The park does not let you down if you're looking for sheer visual enjoyment, with highlights including the Grey Glacier and Mirador Las Torres.

Torres del Paine is accessible year-round, despite the fact that certain parts of Patagonia are inaccessible during the bitter winters.

The park offers a variety of enjoyable activities, but its outstanding hiking paths stand out.

The Patagonia Park

Landscapes and fauna in national parks are often unique or conversation-worthy. Today, however, it is quite uncommon for a new national park to open.

The Patagonia National Park was inaugurated in the Aysén region of southern Chile in 2018. (Parque Patagonia). The park, which was the creation of environmentalist Kristine Thompkins, has become quite well-known.

It is known as the "Serengeti of the Southern Cone" and covers an area of 1,787 sq km at the foot of the Andes Mountains in the Chacabuco River Valley.

I assure you that the nature is truly breathtaking here. To the beautiful Andean condor, uncommon huemul deer, and guanacos that resemble lamas.

Wetlands, mountains, and enormous glacier-fed lakes are just a few of the breathtaking scenery that may be found. These provide the ideal backdrop for wonderful trekking adventures.

The most well-liked track for intrepid travelers is the 23km Lagunas Atlas (or High Lagoons) hike. Large-scale vistas of the Chacabuco Valley and the northern Patagonian ice fields are available on an 8-hour trek close to the tourist center. For a longer and more difficult trip, the three-day, 96 km Avilés to Jeinemeni journey is pure wilderness adventure joy.

Park National Pumalin

After passing past the picturesque village of Hornopirén to the south, the landscape immediately transforms into a labyrinth of beautiful fjörds and little islands. Friends, welcome to Parque Nacional Pumalin. (Pumalin National Park).

Doug and Kristine Thompkins gave Pumalin, once the biggest private nature reserve in the world, to the Chilean government in 2017.

It's one of the biggest in South America, measuring an astounding 2,889 sq km.

Pumalin National Park is the national park in Patagonia that provides the most variety of outdoor activities, if you've ever wondered. Only a boat trip or a multi-day kayak excursion can get you to much of its northern regions (how exciting does that sound?).

The 1,200km long gravel Carretera Austral is a must-see for every wanderlust-filled traveler. It's a well-known multi-day driving or hitchhiking journey that runs from Puerto Montt in Chile's Lake District to Villa O'Higgins.

Park National Queulat

The Queulat National Park (Parque Nacional Queulat), which is situated in Patagonia's Aysén area, spans the Carretera Austral between Coyhaique and Chaitén. It's not one to miss, despite the fact that many tourists ignore it.\

Around 1,500 square kilometers make up Queulat, which is proud to display beautiful woods, craggy mountain peaks, furious rivers, and breathtaking waterfalls.

It also has numerous high-altitude lakes that are encircled by temperate rainforests, which are almost unreal.

Some of the rarest flora, wildflowers, and distinctive creatures may be found in these. You may be wondering at this point why the park is not included on more vacation wish lists. Well, perhaps because it rains virtually nonstop.

However, don't let the weather spoil your party. (literally). If you're ready for some bushwhacking across huge, lush rainforest floors, the park will reward you.

The main reward is found at the Mirador Ventisquero Colgante viewpoint, which is reached after a very short 5.6km climb.

Park Los Glaciares National

I bet there aren't many spots on Earth where you can feel like you're on the edge of the planet.

Los Glaciares National Park in Patagonia, Argentina, is one such location. And that's just the very beginning. (the irony is strong here).

Los Glaciares is without a doubt the most well-known and largest national park in Argentina, with a total area of 7,269 square kilometers. The park is located in the Santa Cruz province of the nation and is often separated into two zones.

The southern parts of the park are first, and they may be reached through the quaint hamlet of El Calafate. Here, sheets of ice in cascading white and blue tones cover the ground.

Of course, none is more laudable than the Perito Moreno glacier, the biggest moving glacier in the world that is accessible on land.

For rock climbers and hikers alike, the rugged Fitz Roy mountain range dominates the scenery at Los Glaciers' northernmost areas. Unsurprisingly, thousands of people utilize El Chaltén, a cosmopolitan town at the base of the mountain, as a base of operations.

National Tierra del Fuego Park Park

Tierra del Fuego, Argentina's southernmost national park, is known by numerous names. Many refer to it as the Land of Fire when translated. Others refer to it as "The End of the World," yet visitors often refer to it as the finest site on Earth.

You'll immediately agree once you set foot on its nearly hypnotic subarctic tundra, which has craggy peaks, Fuegian woods, and gorgeous shoreline.

The parts of Tierra del Fuego that Argentina and Chile both share are those that are easiest to get to.

Beyond its collection of breathtaking scenery, the 630 sq km park serves as a refuge for numerous endangered species.

The Fuegian fox, the amusing Canadian beaver, and an abundance of birds, including condors, call Tierra del Fuego home.

There are several routes to choose from if you want to take advantage of the area's greatest hiking options. The majority of day walks start in Ushuaia, the southernmost city in the world. The 9 km Laguna Esmerelda path is renowned for its relative simplicity and should be finished in 4 to 5 hours.

The three-day Torres del Ro Chico Base Camp Trek, which is difficult and very rewarding, attracts the majority of intrepid hikers. It finishes at a high Andean plateau with amazing views from sea level not far from Ushuaia.

National Park of Nahuel Huapi

The park, which covers an area of 7,122 sq km, is located in Argentina's Lake District not far from Bariloche.

There is no rival to Nahuel Huapi for nature enthusiasts seeking for South America's most picturesque lakes and woods.

Since there are more than 60 lakes and lagoons in the park, water sports take precedence over trekking and mountain climbing, which are strengths of other parks.

These range from simpler activities like swimming and kayaking to more adventurous ones like fly fishing and sailing.

That is not to suggest that the park doesn't provide enough of hiking enjoyment. However, be prepared since the majority of the paths in Nahuel Huapi are challenging hikes.

CHAPTER 4

Dining and Lodging

Choosing the right housing and dining options is essential for ensuring a relaxed and enjoyable trip to Patagonia.

Patagonia offers a range of housing options, from budget hostels and campgrounds to lavish hotels and resorts.

Similar to dining options, there are plenty to pick from, including upscale eateries serving gourmet meals as well as local fare and street food.

By learning about some of the top locations to stay and dine in Patagonia, you can use this book to plan your trip and make the most of your time in this gorgeous location.

The Various Accommodation Options

Patagonia, which is the southernmost region of South America, is renowned for its breathtaking natural scenery, varied fauna, and distinctive culture.

Worldwide travelers flock to the area to experience its untamed grandeur and outdoor activity possibilities. Patagonia provides a broad range of accommodation choices, from simple campsites to five-star lodgings, in order to support this expanding tourist sector.

We'll look at the various accommodation options in Patagonia in this thorough tour.

Hotels: There are a variety of hotels in Patagonia, from modestly priced hostels to opulent resorts. Restaurants, clubs, saunas, and swimming areas are just a few of the many facilities they provide.

The Tierra Patagonia Hotel & Spa, Explora Patagonia Hotel Salto Chico, and Singular Patagonia Hotel are some of the most well-known lodging establishments in the area.

Hotels in Patagonia come in all price ranges, from cheap lodging to lavish resorts. Here are a few of Patagonia's top lodgings:

The Tierra Patagonia Hotel & Spa is a five-star hotel with a spa that is situated in Torres del Paine National Park and provides breathtaking vistas of the nearby scenery.

A full-service gym, eatery, lounge, and outdoor hot baths are available at the motel. Suites and ordinary accommodations are just two of the many options available to visitors.

The Singular Patagonia Hotel is a five-star establishment built in a former refrigerated storage facility and is situated in Puerto Bories on the banks of the Fjord of Last Hope. There is an indoor pool, a gym, a cafeteria, and a lounge at the motel. Suites and ordinary accommodations are just two of the many options available to visitors.

The Torres del Paine National Park's centrally situated Hotel Las Torres Patagonia provides breathtaking vistas of the area.

There are outdoor hot pools, a cafeteria, and a lounge at the motel. Suites and ordinary accommodations are just two of the many options available to visitors.

The luxurious Explora Patagonia Hotel Salto Chico is situated in Torres del Paine National Park on the banks of Lake Pehoé. There are outdoor hot pools, a cafeteria, a lounge, and a gym at the motel. Suites and ordinary accommodations are just two of the many options available to visitors.

Located in Puerto Natales, the Hotel Costaustralis provides breathtaking vistas of the Ultima Esperanza Sound. An eatery, lounge, and indoor pool are available at the motel. Suites and ordinary accommodations are just two of the many options available to visitors.

The world's southernmost metropolis, Ushuaia, is home to the opulent Arakur Ushuaia Resort & Spa.

The motel has an interior pool as well as an outdoor pool, a cafeteria, and a gym. Suites and ordinary accommodations are just two of the many options available to visitors.

Luxury hotel in Ushuaia with breathtaking vistas of the Beagle Channel is called Los Cauquenes Resort & Spa. The motel has an interior pool as well as an outdoor pool, a cafeteria, and a gym. Suites and ordinary accommodations are just two of the many options available to visitors.

Hotel Patagonia Plaza: This lodging facility is situated in El Calafate and provides breathtaking vistas of Lake Argentino.

An eatery, lounge, and indoor pool are available at the motel. Suites and ordinary accommodations are just two of the many options available to visitors.

These are only a few of the numerous lodgings that are offered in Patagonia. Anywhere you remain, you can count on being encircled by breathtaking natural beauty and memorable scenery.

Lodges: Lodges typically have fewer accommodations than motels, a cozier ambiance, and a smaller size. From opulent apartments to rural cottages, they provide a variety of lodging options.

Patagonia has a large number of cabins that are tucked away, giving tourists a rare chance to escape civilization and get close to nature.

The Awasi Patagonia Lodge, Ecocamp Patagonia, and Patagonia Camp are a few of the best hotels in the area.

Hostels: Backpackers and low-cost tourists frequently choose hostels. They provide both individual cabins and inexpensive dormitory-style lodging.

For guests to mingle and unwind, hostels in Patagonia frequently offer shared kitchens and common spaces.

The Refugio Paine Grande, El Chaltén, and Erratic Rock hotels are a few of Patagonia's top hotels.

Cabins: Those who want to take in Patagonia's wild grandeur while still having access to home amenities frequently opt for cabins.

There are all kinds of cabins in the area, from simple, rural lodgings to opulent getaways with fires and hot baths. Los Alamos Cabins, Cabanas Bahia Celeste, and Cabanas del Paine are a few of Patagonia's top lodging options.

Camping is a well-liked activity in Patagonia for enjoying the environment. The area has a range of camping choices, from budget-friendly sites to deluxe ones with facilities like hot baths and power.

A lot of the campgrounds in Patagonia are found in breathtaking natural surroundings, giving guests a one-of-a-kind and memorable experience. The Torres Del Paine Campground, El Chaltén Campground, and Los

Glaciares National Park Campground are a few of the finest campgrounds in the area.

Estancias: Estancias are typical Patagonian farms that provide tourists with an exceptional chance to experience the culture and way of life of the area.

Numerous estancias provide lodging, which can range from modest rural cabins to opulent apartments.

Visitors can take part in events like equestrian riding, livestock butchering, and gaucho performances. Among Patagonia's top estancias are the Estancia Cristina, El Galpón del Glaciar, and Estancia Nibepo Aike.

From simple campsites to five-star lodgings and everything in between, Patagonia provides a wide variety of housing choices.

Every tourist can find something to enjoy in Patagonia, whether they're searching for an opulent getaway or an isolated desert adventure. You will undoubtedly be mesmerized by the area's breathtaking natural scenery and distinctive culture, regardless of the kind of accommodation you pick.

Eateries and Cafés.

There are many dining establishments in Patagonia that serve a wide selection of foods to suit any palate. A detailed list of some of Patagonia's top eateries is provided below:

La Marmita: This restaurant, which is renowned for its modern Patagonian food, is situated in the village of Puerto Natales.

The eatery serves food like king crab, meat that has been prepared slowly, and handmade noodles in a warm, rural setting.

In the village of El Calafate, there is a café and patisserie called Cassis that serves a range of baked goods like croissants, sandwiches, and desserts. There are various coffee and beverage options available at the café.

La Tablita: This El Chalten establishment is renowned for its authentic Argentine barbeque. Along with a selection of proteins like beef, lamb, and pig, the eatery also serves meatless meals.

Morphen: This eatery and pub is situated in Punta Arenas and serves a selection of foreign dishes, such as sushi, sandwiches, and pizza. Craft brews and beverages are also available at the eatery.

La Aldea: This restaurant in the town of Ushuaia is well-known for its shellfish specialties, which include king crab and Patagonian prawns. Views of the Beagle Channel are available, and the eatery has a pleasant atmosphere.

Coffee & Wool: This Puerto Varas coffee shop serves a selection of sandwiches, sweets, and coffee beverages. A variety of locally produced textile goods are also available at the café.

In the village of Puerto Montt, there is an eatery called Kau Kaleshen that serves up typical Chilean fare.

The eatery serves meals like grilled lamb, shellfish soups, and empanadas.

La Cocina is an eatery with a range of Argentine and foreign dishes that is situated in the municipality of San Carlos de Bariloche.

The eatery has a warm atmosphere and serves cuisine like barbecued meats, spaghetti, and shellfish.

In the village of Esquel, there is a café called Café Riquet, which serves a selection of sandwiches, sweets, and coffee beverages. A variety of handmade sweets are also available at the café.

Mirador del Lago: This eatery, which is situated in El Calafate, provides breathtaking vistas of Lake Argentino. Grilled meats, soups, and empanadas are just a few of the Argentine dishes served at the eatery.

You will undoubtedly find an eatery or café in Patagonia that fits your preferences wherever you go.

Patagonia is undoubtedly a food lover's heaven with its wide variety of foods and breath-taking natural beauty.

CHAPTER 5

Cities in Patagonia

Argentina's Ushuaia is the southernmost metropolis in the world and is situated at the southernmost point of South America.

It is referred to as the "End of the World." With chances for snowboarding, trekking, and experiencing the neighboring Tierra del Fuego National Park, it is a well-liked vacation spot for action seekers.

The city is also home to a number of institutions, including the Prison Museum and Maritime Museum, which provide views into the past of the area.

Argentina's Puerto Madryn, on the eastern edge of Patagonia, is well-known for its abundance of aquatic life, which includes whales, sea otters, and penguins. Visitors can take boat excursions to get up-close views of the wildlife at this well-liked wildlife viewing location. A number of artistic institutions, such as the Ecocentro, which examines the maritime ecosystem of the area, are also located in the city.

Argentina's Bariloche is renowned for its breathtaking natural landscape, which includes lakes, mountains, and woods.

Bariloche is situated in the Andes highlands. It is a well-liked location for outdoor pursuits like snowboarding, trekking, and fishing.

The city is also home to a number of confectionery stores that provide a delectable sample of the cuisine of the area.

Punta Arenas, Chile: Punta Arenas is a thriving harbor city that acts as an entryway to Antarctica and is situated on Chile's southernmost point.

The area of Cerro Alegre is renowned for its colorful homes and ancient design. The Magellan Strait and Torres del Paine National Park are just two of the local natural sites that tourists can experience.

Puerto Varas, Chile: This lakeside city is well-known for its German-inspired building and breathtaking vistas of the Osorno and Calbuco mountains. It is situated on the banks of Lake Llanquihue.

Outdoor pursuits like fly fishing, paddling, and trekking are very common there. Numerous artistic institutions, such as the Pablo Fierro Museum, which exhibits the work of regional artists, are also located in the city.

Argentina's El Calafate is renowned for its magnificent glaciers, including the Perito Moreno Glacier, a UNESCO World Heritage Site.

The town of El Calafate is located in the southern part of Argentine Patagonia. Visitors can take boat excursions to get up-close views of the glaciers or visit the Los Glaciares National Park and other local natural wonders.

Chile's Puerto Montt, which is famous for its shellfish and regional dishes, is situated on the Reloncav Sound's beaches. Outdoor pursuits like snowboarding, canoeing, and trekking are very common there. The city is also home to a number of institutions, such as the Juan Pablo II Museum, which presents the past of the indigenous civilizations in the area.

No matter where you go in Patagonia, you'll discover a community that provides a special fusion of outdoor excitement, cultural legacy, and natural beauty.

Patagonia is undoubtedly a place that piques curiosity and encourages travel due to its expansive and varied environments.

CHAPTER 6

Hiking in Patagonia

Hiking Trails

An array of trekking choices, from day treks to multi-day loops, are available in Torres del Paine National Park in Chile, one of the most well-known trekking locations in Patagonia.

The "W" Circuit, which takes about 4-5 days to finish and provides breathtaking vistas of the park's glaciers, lakes, and mountains, is the most well-known journey.

Los Glaciares National Park in Argentina is a well-liked location for hiking and provides a number of trekking paths, including the renowned Fitz Roy Trek and the Cerro Torre Trek. Both hikes are doable in 4-5 days and provide breathtaking vistas of the park's mountains and ice.

Tierra del Fuego National Park in Argentina: This park, which is at the southernmost point of South America, has a number of hiking trails, including the Coastal Trek and Pampa Alta Trek.

Both hikes last two to three days and provide breathtaking vistas of the park's rocky shoreline, woods, and lakes.

Trekking Equipment

- Hiking footwear: For walking in Patagonia, you must have a decent set of hiking footwear. Choose footwear with excellent heel support, durability, and weather resistance.
- When hiking in Patagonia, it's important to layer up because the weather can change quickly. Bring a fleece or down parka, a cap, mittens, and a weatherproof garment.

- Bag: To transport your supplies, sustenance, and drink, you will need a reliable bag. Find a bag that is both comfortable to wear and has enough room for your belongings.
- Shelter and sleeping bag: If you intend to go camping, you'll need a sturdy shelter and comfortable bedding. A strong, weatherproof shelter and a toasty, portable camping blanket are things to look for.

Preparation:

- Fitness: Trekking in Patagonia can be difficult, so it's crucial to be in top physical condition before you go.
- Start your preparations months in advance of your journey, concentrating on both muscle and aerobic conditioning.

- Weather: With strong gusts, rain, and snow, the weather in Patagonia can be erratic. Bring weatherproof tools and comfortable apparel so you can be ready for any conditions.
- Permissions: Check in advance and secure any required permissions before you travel because some hiking paths in Patagonia require them.
- A first aid pack, a map and guide, a satellite phone, and an emergency signal should all be brought when trekking in Patagonia because of the potential for peril.

Trekking in Patagonia is a unique experience that provides breathtaking views, difficult topography, and a chance to get close to nature.

You can start on a hiking journey that will last a lifetime with the proper planning and equipment.

CHAPTER 7

Culture of Patagonia

Argentina and Chile are included in the extensive and varied area known as Patagonia. The region has a diverse and complex culture that has been influenced by many indigenous groups and millennia of history.

History:

Patagonia has a protracted and intricate past that goes back thousands of years. The Tehuelche, the Mapuche, and the Selk'nam were among the original peoples who first occupied the area.

The area underwent major transformations following the entrance of European explorers and colonists in the 16th century, including the spread of illness, the introduction of Christianity, and the eviction of native populations.

Following this, Argentina and Chile engaged in numerous territorial disputes over Patagonia, with both nations ultimately asserting ownership of portions of the area.

Indigenous Peoples:

With centuries of history and the impact of numerous other groups, the indigenous people of Patagonia have developed a rich and complex society.

The Mapuche, the Selk'nam, and the Tehuelche are some of the most well-known tribal tribes in the area.

Prior to the advent of Europeans, the Tehuelche people were a migratory group of hunters and gatherers in Patagonia.

They were expert hunters who took down big beasts like guanacos and rheas with bows and arrows. The Mapuche people, who are mainly found in Chile, have a lively and rich culture that combines traditional music and dance with a strong sense of connection to the environment.

The Selk'nam people, who once inhabited southern Patagonia, are famous for their elaborate cave drawings and their dead language.

Celebrations and Festivals:

Numerous gatherings and events are held throughout Patagonia to honor the area's diverse cultural history. Among the most well-known events are:

- The Festival of the water (Fiesta del Mar), which takes place in September in Puerto Madryn, honors the area's ties to the water. It features a variety of cultural activities, such as displays of traditional music and dance, seafood sampling, and boat competitions.
- The National Sheep Festival (Fiesta Nacional del Cordero), which takes place in Puerto Madryn in November, honors the history of sheep herding in

the area. Shearing contests, traditional food tastings, and cultural shows are all part of it.

- The national festival known as Indigenous Peoples Day (Da de los Pueblos Originarios), which is observed on August 11, honors all of Argentina's indigenous civilizations, including those from Patagonia. It consists of instructional activities, traditional cuisine tastings, and cultural shows.

Patagonia is a place with a lively indigenous legacy that is still discernible today. Patagonia is an area that is rich in variety and complexity, from the nomadic hunters of the Tehuelche to the lively cultural customs of the Mapuche and Selk'nam.

Patagonia continues to flourish and develop while keeping its rich cultural legacy for future generations by honoring its indigenous cultures and enjoying its festivals.

CHAPTER 8

Hints and Concluding Suggestions

Although it takes some planning and preparation, visiting Patagonia can be an amazing experience. For anyone considering a journey to this breathtaking area, here are some last-minute advice and transport suggestions:

- Learn about the weather in Patagonia and prepare appropriately. There are many different types of weather there, from mild and sunny to chilly and rainy. When packing, make sure to include layers, waterproof clothing, and durable hiking footwear. It's important to study the weather for the time of year you plan to travel.

- Due to Patagonia's size and abundance of attractions, make a travel plan. Planning your schedule in preparation is a good idea, so consider things like travel, lodging, and activities. There is no lack of breathtaking landscape and outdoor activities in the region, so be sure to allot enough time to explore it thoroughly.
- If you are unfamiliar with the region, think about signing up for a guided trip. Whether you're interested in trekking, wildlife viewing, or cultural encounters, a native guide can offer insightful information and show you the finest places.
- Respect the environment: The delicate ecology of Patagonia needs cautious preservation. When trekking or camping, it's critical to honor nature and adhere to the Leave No Trace philosophy. Do

not disturb animals, remain on designated paths, and don't litter.
- Study the local culture: Patagonia is home to a rich and varied culture that includes indigenous peoples and newcomers from Europe. Respect local traditions by taking the time to educate yourself on the history and habits of the region.
- Because Patagonia is a vast area, lengthy distances may be involved when journeying between locations. Whether you plan to hire a vehicle or take the bus, make sure to arrange your transportation appropriately.

In general, Patagonia is a secure place to visit, but it's still important to exercise prudence by avoiding remote areas, being mindful of your surroundings, and never leaving assets unguarded.

Those who enjoy outdoor activities, gorgeous landscapes, and vibrant cultural customs may find visiting Patagonia to be an unforgettable experience. You can maximize your journey while honoring the environment and regional traditions by heeding the advice and suggestions in this guide.

Prepare yourself for the journey of a lifetime in Patagonia by packing your bags and lacing up your hiking footwear.

Conclusion

There is something for every kind of tourist in Patagonia, making it a once-in-a-lifetime adventure. This area offers everything you could possibly want, whether it be excitement, leisure, or cultural experience. Patagonia genuinely has something for everyone, with its breathtaking glaciers, mountains, animals, and cultural legacy.

Patagonia's natural grandeur, which is unmatched anywhere else in the world, is one of its biggest attractions. The extensive landscapes with their majestic summits, clear lakes, and old glaciers are breathtaking and will surely leave you speechless.

As a result of the region's abundance of wildlife, which includes condors, guanacos, and pumas, it is a popular location for those who enjoy the outdoors.

Patagonia is a region rich in natural beauty as well as history and culture.

The area is home to a mixed population of indigenous and foreign groups, each with its own distinctive traditions and rituals.

Visitors can gain intriguing insight into the people who call Patagonia home by learning about the region's history and cultural legacy through museums, celebrations, and encounters with locals.

It takes some planning and preparation to travel to Patagonia, but the work is well worth it. Careful preparation will ensure you have the journey of a lifetime, from picking the best season to visit to picking the best trekking routes and lodgings.

All things considered, Patagonia is the ideal location if you're searching for a place that provides breathtaking natural beauty, a variety of cultural encounters, and outdoor adventures. Then why wait?

Plan your trip now, and get set to experience this breathtaking area like never before.

Made in the USA
Las Vegas, NV
25 September 2023

78133573R00046